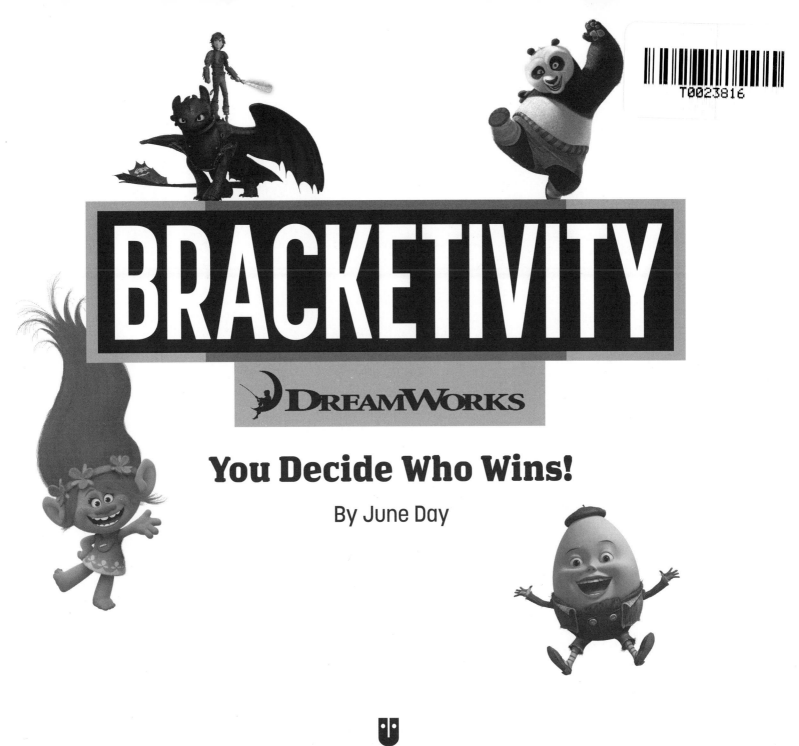

BRACKETIVITY

DreamWorks

You Decide Who Wins!

By June Day

Andrews McMeel
PUBLISHING®

Andrews McMeel Publishing
a division of Andrews McMeel Universal
1130 Walnut Street, Kansas City, Missouri 64106

www.andrewsmcmeel.com

23 24 25 26 27 RLP 10 9 8 7 6 5 4 3 2 1

ISBN: 978-1-5248-8580-9

Editor: Erinn Pascal
Art Director: Tiffany Meairs
Production Editor: Meg Utz
Production Manager: Tamara Haus

Made by:
Shenzhen Reliance Printing Co., Ltd.
Address and place of manufacturer:
25 Longshan Industrial Zone, Nanling,
Longgang District, Shenzhen, China, 518114
1st Printing – 5/15/23

ATTENTION: SCHOOLS AND BUSINESSES

Andrews McMeel books are available at quantity discounts with bulk purchase for educational, business, or sales promotional use. For information, please e-mail the Andrews McMeel Publishing Special Sales Department: sales@amuniversal.com.

BRACKETIVITY

DreamWorks

**DreamWorks Animation films and TV shows are the best of the best—
just ask Shrek, who knows a thing or two about blockbuster adventures.**

In your hands is a very special DreamWorks-themed Bracketivity book. Within these pages, you'll be able to pick your favorite "thing" in each category. But it's not just a "pick and go" situation—you'll have to fill each bracket to determine your winner!

Think about each answer carefully, because it determines your next round of brackets. Or go with your gut feeling—really, there's no wrong answer! And at the end of the book, you'll even get to make your own Bracketivities to share with family and friends.

As Donkey says, "This is gonna be fun!"

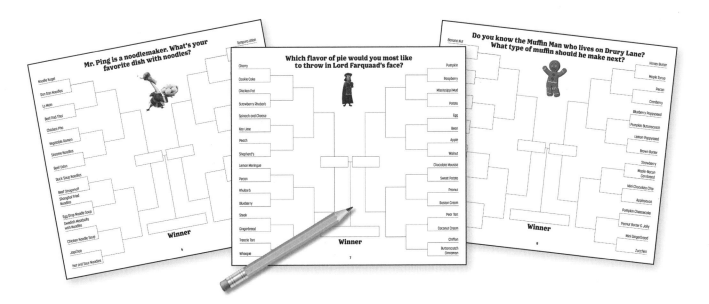

Skipper is a big-time leader. What's your dream job?

Singer

Lawyer — Lawyer

Book Editor — Book Editor

Computer Programmer — Book Editor

BRACKETIVITY EXAMPLE

Here's an example **Bracketivity** that's filled out. It's what the author would pick. Don't worry—if you disagree, you'll get to fill out your own **Bracketivities** on the next page.

Actor

Actor — Actor

Physicist

Football Player

Painter — Painter

Painter

Chef

Chef — Chef

Firefighter

Teacher

Doctor

Teacher — Teacher

Teacher

Book Editor — Book Editor

Librarian

Actor

Librarian

Librarian — Librarian

Musician

Librarian

CEO

CEO — CEO

Astronomer

Airplane Pilot

Veterinarian — Veterinarian

Veterinarian

Author

Author — Author

Biologist — Author

Author

Author — Author

Mayor

TikTok Star — TikTok Star

TikTok Star

Judge

Judge — Judge

Soccer Player

Author — **Therapist**

Vlogger

Accountant

Vlogger — Vlogger

Vlogger

Vlogger

Race Car Driver

Zoologist — Zoologist

Zoologist

Therapist

Engineer

Nurse — Nurse

Nurse

Therapist

Therapist

Therapist — Therapist

President

Author
Winner

Skipper is a big-time leader. What's your dream job?

Singer

Lawyer

Book Editor

Computer Programmer

Chef

Firefighter

Doctor

Teacher

Airplane Pilot

Veterinarian

Author

Biologist

Mayor

TikTok Star

Judge

Soccer Player

Actor

Physicist

Football Player

Painter

Librarian

Musician

CEO

Astronomer

Accountant

Vlogger

Race Car Driver

Zoologist

Engineer

Nurse

Therapist

President

Winner

Mr. Ping is a noodlemaker. What's your favorite dish with noodles?

Noodle Kugel

Dan Dan Noodles

Lo Mein

Beef Pad Thai

Chicken Pho

Vegetable Ramen

Sesame Noodles

Beef Udon

Duck Soup Noodles

Beef Stroganoff

Shanghai Fried Noodles

Egg Drop Noodle Soup

Swedish Meatballs with Noodles

Chicken Noodle Soup

Japchae

Hot and Sour Noodles

Tempura Udon

Curry Noodles

Wonton Noodles

Vegetable Chow Mein

Glass Noodle Soup

Spaetzle

Beef Chow Fun

Tofu Pad Thai

Pork Udon

Fried Rice Noodles

Buttered Noodles

Seafood Ramen

Zucchini Noodles

Garlic Noodles

Tuna Casserole

Yaki Udon

Winner

Which flavor of pie would you most like to throw in Lord Farquaad's face?

Cherry

Cookie Cake

Chicken Pot

Strawberry Rhubarb

Spinach and Cheese

Key Lime

Peach

Shepherd's

Lemon Meringue

Pecan

Rhubarb

Blueberry

Steak

Gingerbread

Treacle Tart

Whoopie

Pumpkin

Raspberry

Mississippi Mud

Potato

Egg

Bean

Apple

Walnut

Chocolate Mousse

Sweet Potato

Peanut

Boston Cream

Pear Tart

Coconut Cream

Chiffon

Butterscotch Cinnamon

Winner

Do you know the Muffin Man who lives on Drury Lane?
What type of muffin should he make next?

Banana Nut

Blueberry

Carrot

Cornbread

Chocolate Chip

Pumpkin Spice

Strawberry Cheesecake

Apple Cinnamon

Blueberry Lemon Poppyseed

Triple Chocolate

Gingerbread

Cranberry Orange

Chocolate Chip Pumpkin

Blueberry Yogurt

Egg

Lemon

Honey Butter

Maple Syrup

Pecan

Cranberry

Blueberry Poppyseed

Pumpkin Butterscotch

Lemon Poppyseed

Brown Butter

Strawberry

Maple-Bacon Cornbread

Mini Chocolate Chip

Applesauce

Pumpkin Cheesecake

Peanut Butter & Jelly

Mini Gingerbread

Zucchini

Winner

Gingy is about to decorate his gingerbread house!
What's your favorite part about the holidays?

Holiday Lights

Family

Opening Presents

Cutting Down a Christmas Tree

Putting Up Your Stocking

Holiday Music

Snow

No School

Gingerbread Cookies

Playing Dreidel

Stocking Stuffers

Giving Presents

Eating Latkes

Decorating a Gingerbread House

The Yule Bonfire

Making Holiday Cookies

Lighting Candles

Reindeer

Sitting by the Fireplace

Waking Up on Christmas Morning

Shopping for Presents

Holiday Movies

Singing Carols

Decorating the Christmas Tree

Praying

Visiting Family

Holiday Parties

Big Holiday Meals

School Snow Days

Making Ornaments for the Tree

Family Traditions

Making Cookies for Santa Claus

Winner

Jack Frost can create frost on any object he touches!
What's the best part about winter?

Snow!

Being Cozy Inside

Sledding

A Big, Warm Coat

Snow Days

Skiing

Hot Cocoa

Ice Skating

Wearing Earmuffs

Butternut Squash Soup

Christmas

Snowshoeing

Colorful Scarves

Snuggling Under a Blanket

Making Snow Angels

Snowboarding

Watching the Snow Fall

Wearing Winter Caps

Building a Snowperson

Drinking Hot Tea

Catching Snowflakes on Your Tongue

New Year's Eve Celebration

Pumpkin Pie

Chicken Noodle Soup

Hanukkah

School Winter Break

Waking Up to Fresh Snow

Fire in the Fireplace

Holiday Lights

Wearing Mittens

Snowball Fights

Matzo Ball Soup

Winner

The *Madagascar* crew journeyed to many places! Of these, which city would you most like to visit?

Johannesburg, South Africa

Beijing, China

Brussels, Belgium

Cairo, Egypt

Rome, Italy

Buenos Aires, Argentina

Athens, Greece

Shanghai, China

New Delhi, India

Addis Ababa, Ethiopia

Amsterdam, The Netherlands

Moscow, Russia

Los Angeles, California

Tokyo, Japan

Kathmandu, Nepal

Sydney, Australia

Chicago, Illinois

Bali, Indonesia

Reykjavik, Iceland

Quito, Ecuador

Dublin, Ireland

Madrid, Spain

Rio de Janeiro, Brazil

Casablanca, Morocco

London, United Kingdom

Paris, France

Munich, Germany

Mexico City, Mexico

New York City, New York

Oslo, Norway

Osaka, Japan

Honolulu, Hawaii

Winner

The New York Zoo is a super popular spot in *Madagascar*— just ask Mort! What's your favorite animal to visit at the zoo?

Lions

Grizzly Bears

Dolphins

Red Pandas

Tigers

Gorillas

Turtles

Polar Bears

Hippopotamuses

Capybaras

Flamingos

Giraffes

Penguins

Zebras

Crocodiles

Sea Lions

Gazelles

Rhinoceroses

Lemurs

Cheetahs

Elephants

Camels

Panda Bears

Anacondas

Chimpanzees

Komodo Dragons

Prairie Dogs

Peacocks

Axolotls

Bats

Orangutans

Foxes

Winner

Megamind is a super-smart supervillain. What's the best superpower to have?

X-Ray Vision

Invisibility

Flying

Mind-Reading

Super-Speed

Controlling Water

Super-Intelligence

Shapeshifting Yourself

Telekinesis

Controlling Fire

Teleportation

Super-Vision

Elasticity

Vocal Mind Control

Super-Hearing

Shapeshifting Other Objects

Hypnosis

Talking to Animals

Master of Disguise

Reality Warping

Super-Immunity

Magical Abilities

Time Travel

Manipulating Rocks and Dirt

Sonic Scream

Duplicating Yourself

Night Vision

Healing

Manipulating Air and Wind

Breathing Underwater

Memory Manipulation

Voice Manipulation

Winner

The Trolls love to sing, dance, and hug—all the time! What kind of party would you like to plan with the Trolls?

Masquerade Ball

'80s Party

Tea Party

Dance Party

Wacky Hair Party

Cake Tasting Party

Pirates Party

Surprise Party

Black-Tie Party

Holiday Party

Funny Hat Party

Black Light Party

Potluck Party

Fantasy Character Party

Garden Party

Sleepover Party

'50s Party

Funny Costume Party

Karaoke Party

Boardgame Party

Pizza Party

DreamWorks Character Costume Party

Halloween Party

Mermaid Party

Sports Party

Circus Party

Baking Party

Nautical-Themed Party

Picnic Party

Scavenger Hunt Party

Camping Party

Pool Party

Winner

When in disguise, Puss In Boots went by the name Pickles. What's the best name for a cat?

Lily

Lorna

Pickles

Wolfie

Sweet Pea

Parsnip

Bonkerton

Pandy Paws

Kitty

Gordo

Marshmallow

Cakey

Gus

Spooky

Floyd

Mack

DJ Catnip

Grover

Princess

Claude

Whiskers

Sebastian

Mr. Sandwiches

Stella

MerCat

Zing

Jinx

Barnabas

Toby

Snuggles

Tank

Biscuit

Winner

Donkey is making waffles!
What's the best waffle topping?

Strawberries

Cinnamon and Sugar

Bananas

Whipped Cream

Peaches

Maple Syrup

Vanilla Ice Cream

Raspberries

Blackberries

Chocolate Chips

Strawberry Ice Cream

Honey

Peanut Butter

Bacon

Chocolate Hazelnut Spread

Fried Chicken

Winner

Chocolate Sprinkles

Oranges

Walnuts

Boysenberries

Cherries

Another Waffle!

Granola

Lemon Glaze

Eggs

Butter

Apples

Rainbow Sprinkles

Chocolate Ice Cream

Pecans

Marshmallows

Caramel

Poppy and Branch are hosting a singing competition! What are you singing?

Rock & Roll

Wedding Music

Bluegrass

Country

Dance Pop

Folk Punk

Grunge

Hard Rock

Yodel

Anime

Rap

Holiday Music

Pop Punk

Disco

Classic Blues

Broadway

Contemporary R&B

Jazz

Metal

Lullabye

Reggae

Soft Rock

Opera

Country Pop

Techno

Folk

Sung Poetry

Hip-Hop

K-Pop

Samba

Motown

Movie Soundtrack

Winner

King Julien loves mangoes—one time, he inadvertently created a giant mango that tried to take over the world! Of these, what's your favorite?

Cantaloupe

Pear

Apple

Strawberry

Kiwi

Peach

Avocado

Honeydew

Blueberry

Pumpkin

Orange

Passionfruit

Lemon

Tomato

Watermelon

Grapes

Durian

Tangerine

Lime

Blackberry

Banana

Pomegranate

Cherry

Red Pepper

Grapefruit

Mango

Apricot

Jackfruit

Pineapple

Raspberry

Guava

Nectarine

Winner

In *Abominable*, Yi goes to Mount Everest. If you could go anywhere with her, where would it be?

Art Museum

Robotics Lab

Ballet Performance

Animal Shelter Tour

Baseball Game

Natural History Museum

Play

Children's Museum

State Capital Building Tour

Amusement Park

Pumpkin Patch

Golf Course

Renaissance Faire

Magic Show

Presidential Library

Fire Station Tour

Zoo

Musical Theatre Performance

Cooking Class

History Museum

Indoor Skydiving Park

Science Center

Indoor Water Park

Opera

Football Stadium Tour

Orchestra Performance

City Monument Tour

Hands-on Art Class

Wildlife Center

Botanical Gardens

Indoor Trampoline Park

Circus

Winner

Hiccup and his friends learn to train dragons at the Berk Dragon Training Academy. What's your favorite school subject?

American Sign Language

Social Studies

Algebra

World History

Earth Science

Political Science

English

Computers

Lunch

Botany

Spanish

Astronomy

Mythology

Drama

Biology

Latin

French

Economics

Reading

Choir

Physics

Geometry

Pottery

Robotics

Philosophy

Mandarin

Journalism

Woodworking

Chemistry

Photography

Gym

Study Hall

Winner

B.O.B. is the product of a genetically altered tomato and a ranch-flavored dessert. What's your favorite vegetable or plant?

Celery

Radish

Carrots

Broccoli

Collard Greens

Artichoke

Cauliflower

Cabbage

Brussel Sprouts

Asparagus

Bok Choy

Onion

Garlic

Lima Bean

Scallions

Mushroom

Yam

Zucchini

Kale

Spaghetti Squash

Endive Lettuce

Green Beans

Beet

Chard

Potato

Turnip

Baby Broccoli

Rutabaga

Shallot

Corn

Daikon

Eggplant

Winner

Master Oogway is excellent at kung fu, a martial art and full-combat sport. What's the best sport?

Golfing

Swimming

Equestrian

Volleyball

Sailing

Judo

Soccer / Football

Table Tennis

Diving

Archery

Gymnastics

Fencing

Track and Field

Basketball

Boxing

Water Polo

Figure Skating

Bobsledding

Alpine Skiing

Weightlifting

Canoeing

Snowboarding

Surfing

Rowing

Ice Hockey

Trampoline

Cheerleading

Ice Dancing

Ski Jumping

Mountain Biking

Karate

Wrestling

Winner

Bridget and King Gristle Jr. go on a date for pizza. What pizza topping should they get?

Anchovies

Canadian Bacon

Mozzarella

Pineapple

Pepperoni

Banana Pepper

Black Olives

Ham

Mushroom

Extra Cheese

Garlic

Ground Beef

Onion

Peanut Butter

Bacon

Arugula

Chicken

Green Pepper

Sausage

Tomatoes

Green Olives

Jalapeños

Corn

Artichoke

Hot Sauce

BBQ Sauce

Shrimp

Basil

Prosciutto

Cheddar

Eggs

Goat Cheese

Winner

Imagine you are a Dragon Rider living in Berk. What color or pattern of dragon would you want to ride?

Neon Pink

Cerulean

Black and White

Silver

Violet

Orange

Forest Green

Sand

Purple

Sparkly Gold

Dark Blue

Neon Green

Sky Blue

Rainbow

Orange and Black

Charcoal Gray

Cheetah Print

Light Pink

Turquoise

Zebra Striped

Red

Lavender

Black

Cow Print

Yellow

Silver and Purple

Rose Gold

Brown Spotted

Magenta

Goldenrod

Weathered Gray

Maroon

Winner

Po loves dumplings!
What's your go-to snack after school?

Cookies and Cream

Trail Mix

Banana

Peanut Butter and Jelly Sandwich

Avocado Toast

Chips and Salsa

Lollipop

Fruit Smoothie

Pizza Rolls

Yogurt

Apple

Cheese and Crackers

Peanuts

Ham Sandwich

Chocolate Bar

Carrots and Hummus

Chicken and Rice

Popcorn

Walnuts

Cereal

Protein Bar

Grilled Cheese

Tangerine

Dumplings

Almonds

Empanadas

Chocolate Chip Cookies

Rainbow Candy

Pierogis

Toast with Cinnamon

Dinner Leftovers

Green Juice

Winner

The residents of Trolls Village love to perform! If you were partaking in a talent competition, what would you do?

Classical Opera

Tap Dancing

Playing Flute

Baton Twirling

Performing in a Band

Acrobatics

Playing the Violin

Jazz Dancing

Yo-Yo Tricks

Skateboarding

Performing a Scene from a Play

Miming

Roller Skating

Cooking

Karaoke

Spoken Word Poetry

Painting a Picture

Singing a Pop Song

Trapeze

Performing a Magic Show

Playing the Piano

Interpretive Dance

Rapping

Stand-Up Comedy

Plate-Spinning

Break Dancing

Ventriloquism

Recite the First 50 Digits of Pi

Juggling

Cheerleading

Playing Guitar

Doing a Monologue

Winner

Fiona has a cute Bichon Frisé puppy. Of these, what's the best dog breed?

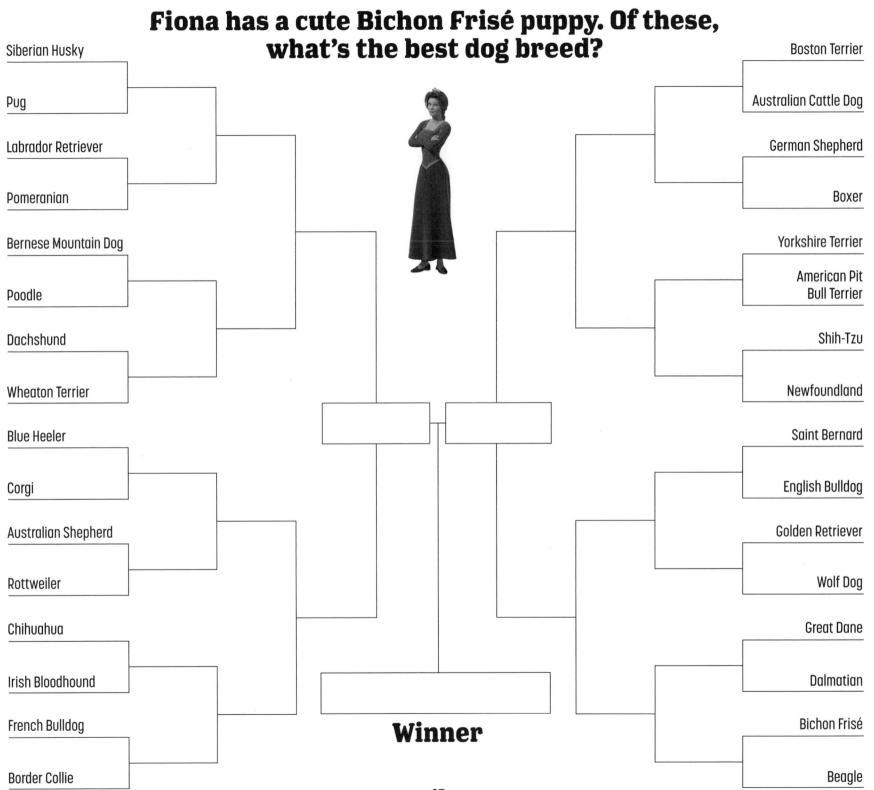

Siberian Husky

Pug

Labrador Retriever

Pomeranian

Bernese Mountain Dog

Poodle

Dachshund

Wheaton Terrier

Blue Heeler

Corgi

Australian Shepherd

Rottweiler

Chihuahua

Irish Bloodhound

French Bulldog

Border Collie

Boston Terrier

Australian Cattle Dog

German Shepherd

Boxer

Yorkshire Terrier

American Pit Bull Terrier

Shih-Tzu

Newfoundland

Saint Bernard

English Bulldog

Golden Retriever

Wolf Dog

Great Dane

Dalmatian

Bichon Frisé

Beagle

Winner

Jin's cousin Peng LOVES to play basketball.
What's your favorite sport or activity?

Baseball

Chess

Diving

Skiing

Lacrosse

Archery

Yoga

Basketball

Ballet

Ice Hockey

Horseback Riding

Rugby

Tennis

Gymnastics

E-Sports

Taekwondo

Track and Field

Soccer

Karate

Cricket

Jazz Dance

Field Hockey

Rock Climbing

Football

Rhythmic Gymnastics

Golf

Cross-Country Running

Snowboarding

Swimming

Weightlifting

Judo

Volleyball

Winner

Pig the cat loves ice cream!
What's your favorite flavor?

Strawberry Cheesecake

Butter Pecan

Chocolate Chip

Vanilla

Salted Caramel

Rum Raisin

Moose Tracks

White Chocolate Raspberry

Mint Chocolate Chip

Coconut

Peaches and Cream

Peanut Butter

Mango Sorbet

Neapolitan

Blueberry

Cinnamon Roll

Tutti Frutti

Bubblegum

Chocolate

Tiramisu

Maple Bacon

Cookie Dough

Rocky Road

Cookies and Cream

Strawberry

Cotton Candy

S'mores

Chocolate Hazelnut

Blackberry Crumble

Creme Brûlée

Strawberry Sorbet

Banana Nut

Winner

Shrek is an ogre, so he likes to eat weedrat and other foods you probably wouldn't. What's your *least* favorite food?

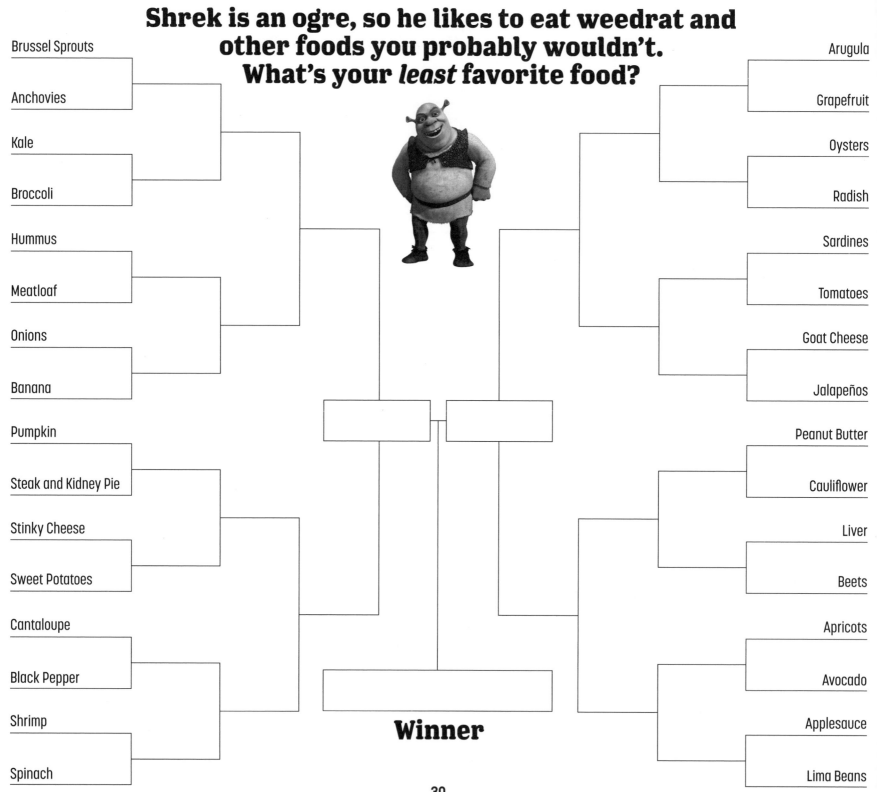

Brussel Sprouts

Anchovies

Kale

Broccoli

Hummus

Meatloaf

Onions

Banana

Pumpkin

Steak and Kidney Pie

Stinky Cheese

Sweet Potatoes

Cantaloupe

Black Pepper

Shrimp

Spinach

Arugula

Grapefruit

Oysters

Radish

Sardines

Tomatoes

Goat Cheese

Jalapeños

Peanut Butter

Cauliflower

Liver

Beets

Apricots

Avocado

Applesauce

Lima Beans

Winner

Donkey thinks he makes a *great* sidekick.
Which mythical creature would you want to be your sidekick?

Unicorn

Griffin

Dragon

Mermaid

Werewolf

Centaur

Bigfoot

Loch Ness Monster

Pegasus

Gnome

Basilisk

Troll

Leprechaun

Jackalope

Sphinx

Hippogriff

Banshee

Flying Monkey

Minotaur

Yeti

Chimera

Phoenix

Ogre

Abominable Snowman

Fairy

Cerberus

Hydra

Chupacabra

Ghoul

Kraken

Vampire

Sea Serpent

Winner

Write in your own:

With the following prompt, fill in your own Bracketivity!

Cats like Puss In Boots have nine lives. But they should still live every life like it's their last! Write down everything on your "bucket list" and then decide which one you're most excited about. A bucket list is all the cool things you want to do in your life!

Winner

Which of these DreamWorks characters would most likely be voted class president at school?

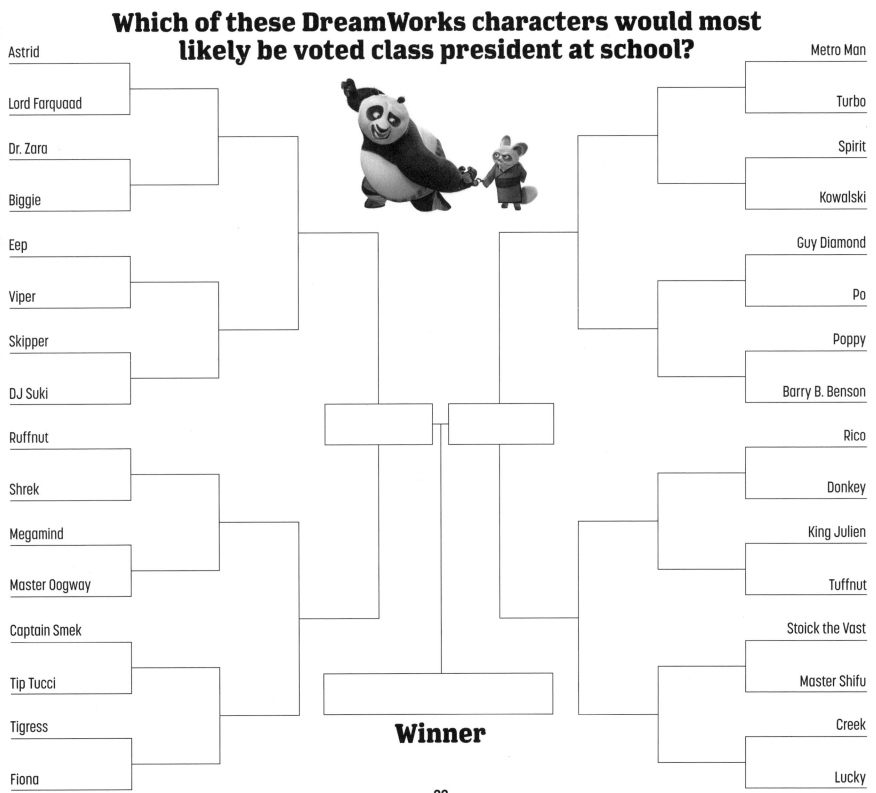

Astrid

Lord Farquaad

Dr. Zara

Biggie

Eep

Viper

Skipper

DJ Suki

Ruffnut

Shrek

Megamind

Master Oogway

Captain Smek

Tip Tucci

Tigress

Fiona

Metro Man

Turbo

Spirit

Kowalski

Guy Diamond

Po

Poppy

Barry B. Benson

Rico

Donkey

King Julien

Tuffnut

Stoick the Vast

Master Shifu

Creek

Lucky

Winner

In *Abominable,* Yi is a violinist. Which musical instrument would you most like to play?

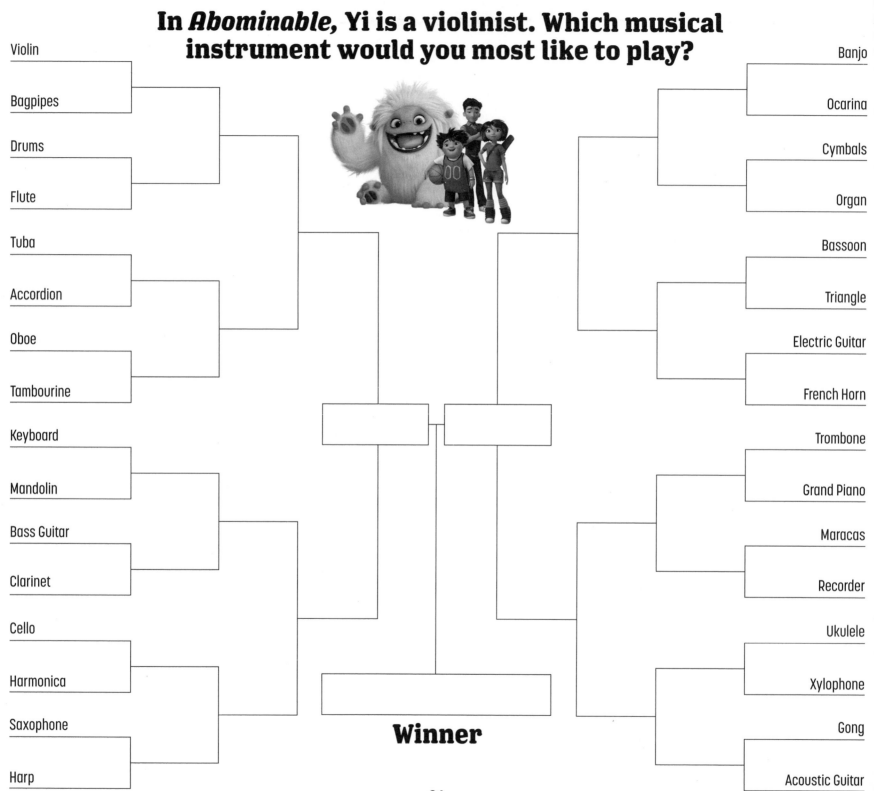

Violin

Bagpipes

Drums

Flute

Tuba

Accordion

Oboe

Tambourine

Keyboard

Mandolin

Bass Guitar

Clarinet

Cello

Harmonica

Saxophone

Harp

Banjo

Ocarina

Cymbals

Organ

Bassoon

Triangle

Electric Guitar

French Horn

Trombone

Grand Piano

Maracas

Recorder

Ukulele

Xylophone

Gong

Acoustic Guitar

Winner

Write in your own:

With the following prompt, fill in your own Bracketivity!

Megamind is a cool name!
Fill in this bracket with all the cool hero
names you would consider naming yourself.
Then, see which one wins!

Winner

The villagers of Berk once feared dragons. Then Hiccup and Toothless showed them they could co-exist. Of these, what's the scariest animal?

Grizzly Bear

Tiger

Shark

Komodo Dragon

Scorpion

Crocodile

Rattlesnake

Hippopotamus

Cougar

Wolf

Sting Ray

Boa Constrictor

Vulture

Swordfish

Sloth Bear

Angler Fish

Puppy

Parakeet

Rhinoceros

Cheetah

Polar Bear

Electric Eel

Mountain Lion

Moose

Piranha

Jellyfish

Bat

Star-Nosed Mole

Tasmanian Devil

Poison Dart Frog

Bull

Anaconda

Winner

Alex the Lion loves summertime—it reminds him of the hot plains in Africa. What's the best part about summer?

No School

Going to the Pool

Bonfires

Camping Trips

Hanging Out with Friends

Riding Bikes

Wearing Shorts

Working a Summer Job

Iced Tea

Hiking

Fireworks

Eating S'mores

Vacation with Your Family

Sleepovers with Your Friends

Picking Berries

Eating Ice Cream

Watching Fireworks

Seeing Fireflies

Summer Camp

Going to the Movies

No Homework

Summer Vegetables

Reading Books

Going to the Beach

Going to the Farmer's Market

Playing Video Games

Climbing Trees

Summer Olympics

Sun Tanning

Nothing! Bring On Winter!

Wearing Flip Flops

Listening to Cicadas

Winner

Who is the evilest villain in the DreamWorks universe?

Lord Farquaad (*Shrek*)

Captain DuBois (*Madagascar*)

Pitch Black (*Rise of the Guardians*)

Kai (*Kung Fu Panda 3*)

Grimmel (*How to Train Your Dragon: The Hidden World*)

Layton T. Montgomery (*Bee Movie*)

Jack Horner (*Puss In Boots: The Last Wish*)

Fairy Godmother (*Shrek 2*)

Lord Shen (*Kung Fu Panda 2*)

Missing Link (*Monsters vs. Aliens*)

Captain Hook (*Shrek the Third*)

Chef (*Trolls*)

The Spiny Mandrilla (*The Croods: A New Age*)

Jack & Jill (*Puss In Boots*)

Dr. Blowhole (*The Penguins of Madagascar*)

Gallaxhar (*Monsters vs. Aliens*)

Metro Man (*Megamind*)

Tai Lung (*Kung Fu Panda*)

Wolf (*Puss In Boots: The Last Wish*)

The Red Death (*How to Train Your Dragon*)

Tighten (*Megamind*)

Dr. Zara (*Abominable*)

Rumpel Stiltskin (*Shrek Forever After*)

Rapunzel (*Shrek the Third*)

Captain Smek (*Home*)

The Fossas (*Madagascar*)

Humpty Alexander Dumpty (*Puss In Boots*)

Queen Barb (*Trolls World Tour*)

Guy Gagne (*Turbo*)

Hendricks (*Spirit: Untamed*)

Drago Bludvist (*How to Train Your Dragon 2*)

Sta'abi (*Monsters vs. Aliens*)

Winner

Write in your own:

With the following prompt, fill in your own Bracketivity!

Write in all *your* favorite DreamWorks characters—then see which one is your favorite of ALL TIME!

Winner

Perro thinks dogs are some of the cutest animals, of course!
What do *you* think is the cutest animal?

Squirrel

Naked Mole Rat

Rabbit

Sloth

Penguin

Kitten

Bear Cub

Deer

Quokka

Jellyfish

Horse

Sea Otter

Capybara

Red Panda (like Master Shifu)

Elephant

Axolotl

Puppy

Raccoon

Piglet

Kiwi Bird

Koala Bear

Hippopotamus

Cow

Fox

Alpaca

Goldfish

Gerbil

Goat

Hedgehog

Puffin

Lemur (like King Julien!)

Chicken

Winner

Write in your own:

With the following prompt, fill in your own Bracketivity!

Turbo dreams of being a racer. What's your dream? Write down 32 dreams and see which one you'd most like to pursue!

Winner

Who is the best DreamWorks hero?

Shrek

Yi

Marty the Zebra

Princess Fiona

Everest

Kitty Softpaws

Branch

Puss In Boots

Barry B. Benson

Hiccup Horrendous Haddock III

Melman the Giraffe

Toothless

Po

Grug

Eep

Poppy

Skipper

Jack Frost

Perro

Mr. Ping

Biggie

Megamind

Ginormica

Ruffnut

Hookfang

Astrid

Tuffnut

Li Shan

Donkey

Alex the Lion

Lucky

Stoick the Vast

Winner

Imagine your Megamind-style superpower is to duplicate objects. If you could have an unlimited number of any of these things, what would it be?

Sneakers

Saturdays

Movies

Books

Cakes

Vacations

Cars

Dogs

Gummy Worms

Cookies

Gift Cards

Clothes

Ice-Cream Cones

Phones

Parties

Pizza

Shirts

Lollipops

Stickers

Gardens

Slippers

Get-Out-of-Homework Passes

Kittens

Computers

Video Games

Action Figures

Cheeseburgers

Lipsticks

Friends

Holiday Presents

Potatoes

TikTok Followers

Winner

In *Monsters vs. Aliens*, a meteor transforms Susan Murphy into Ginormica! What do you think is the coolest part of space?

Tip: If you don't know what something is, look it up!

Asteroids

Earth

Meteors

Aliens

Voltron

Rocket Ships

The Sun

The Moon

Venus

Black Hole

Shooting Star

Dark Energy

Jupiter

Falling Star

The Milky Way

Nebulas

Pluto

The Big Dipper

Mars

The International Space Station

Uranus

Neptune

Antimatter

Comets

Orion

Drones

Saturn

The North Star

Cosmic Dust

Mercury

Quasars

White Dwarf

Winner

The Bee Movie has lots of bees!
Which bug or arachnid is the creepiest?

Weevil

Ant

Bee

Spider

Earwig

Stick Bug

Fire Ant

Flea

Cockroach

Cricket

Stinkbug

Mosquito

Fly

Millipede

Tarantula (like Webs)

Bed Bug

Winner

Wasp

Grasshopper

Firefly

Hornet

Scorpion

Dragonfly

Silverfish

Moth

Scarab Beetle

Worm

Caterpillar

Lady Bug

Cicada

Termite

Daddy Longlegs

Praying Mantis

Which of the Trolls or Bergens do you think would be most likely to go viral in a dance video?

Branch

The K-Pop Gang

Cloud Guy

Biggie

King Gristle Jr.

King Gristle Sr.

Mr. Dinkles

Creek

Mandy Sparkledust

Prince D.

Fuzzbert

Harper

Chef

Queen Barb

Chenille

King Peppy

Bridget

Moxie Dewdrop

Poppy

DJ Suki

Delta Dawn

Guy Diamond

Satin

Grandma Rosiepuff

Smidge

Riff

Tiny Diamond

Cooper

Queen Essence

Cookie Sugarloaf

Legsly

King Thrash

Winner

If you could hang out with any of these DreamWorks animals for the day, who would it be?

Barry B. Benson the bee

Chrome Claw the lobster

Master Oogway the tortoise

Papa Bear the bear

Master Shifu the red panda

Gloria the hippo

Gia the jaguar

Spirit the horse

Master Tigress the tiger

King Julien the lemur

Po the panda

Turbo the snail

Belt the sloth

Dave the octopus

Donkey the donkey

Perro the dog

Mantis the praying mantis

Vitaly the Siberian tiger

Hammy the squirrel

Kowalski the penguin

Lord Shen the peacock

Blowhole the dolphin

Leonard the koala

Viper the snake

Mason the chimpanzee

Eva the snowy owl

Melman the giraffe

Baby Bear the bear

Master Crane the crane

Mooseblood the mosquito

Pig the cat

Stefano the seal

Winner

Imagine these characters are arm (or hoof or paw) wrestling! Who do you think will win?

Jack Horner

Doris

Barry B. Benson

Biggie

Eep

Captain Smek

Toothless

Cinderella

Mort

Meatlug

Humpty Alexander Dumpty

King Julien

Lucky

Yi

Mr. Ping

Megamind

Goldilocks

Grug

Mantis

Dragon (from Shrek)

The Evil Queen

Po

Maurice

B.O.B.

Turbo

Smoove Move

Tigress

Rapunzel

Master Shifu

Spirit

Kitty Softpaws

Astrid

Winner

Cinderella gives Fiona a pooper scooper in *Shrek the Third*. Who should Fiona re-gift it to?

Lancelot

Captain Hook

Dragon

Donkey

Humpty Dumpty

Shrek

Lord Farquaad

Jack Horner

Puss In Boots

Kitty Softpaws

Hansel

Gretel

Big Bad Wolf

King Harold

Jack

Jill

Cookie the Ogre

Mama Bear

Geppetto

The Evil Queen

The Duloc Guards

Doris

Pinocchio

The Muffin Man

Arthur Pendragon

The Fairy Godmother

Prince Charming

Goldilocks

Baby Bear

Gingerbread Man

Grumpy

Queen Lillian

Winner

Big news—your town is now led by a royal!
Who do you hope it is?

King Gristle Jr.

King Gristle Sr.

Stoick the Vast

Prince Charming

Lord Shen

Poppy

Hiccup

Arthur Pendragon

King Quincy

King Trollex

The Evil Queen

Queen Lillian

Mabel

King Julien

Rapunzel

Alex the Lion

King Thrash

Valka

Queen Essence

Princess Fiona

Lord Farquaad

Bridget

King Harold

Queen Barb

Cooper

Prince D.

King Peppy

Toothless

Cinderella

Snow White

Pitch Black

Sleeping Beauty

Winner

Everyone knows that Hiccup rides Toothless, his loyal Night Fury. If you could ride any dragon once, which kind would it be?

Fireworm

Night Terror

Snafflefang

Gronckle

Windstriker

Thunderclaw

Shivertooth

Grim Gnasher

Deadly Nadder

Monstrous Nightmare

Sweet Death

Shadow Wing

Snow Wraith

Bewilderbeast

Night Light

Thunderclaw

Light Fury

Night Fury

Armorwing

Foreverwing

Smothering Smokebreath

Deathgripper

Sentinel

Thunderdrum

Snaptrapper

Flame Whipper

Dramillion

Skrill

Lycanwing

Hideous Zippleback

Rumblehorn

Stormcutter

Winner

Kitty Softpaws wants to make a wish on the Wishing Star. If you could have any of these wishes granted, what would it be?

All-Expenses Paid Trip to France

Unlimited Candy

Make Your Pet Live Forever

No Chores Ever Again

The Ability to Read Peoples' Minds

Meet Your Favorite Celebrity

A New Video Game System

More Friends

Act in a Feature Film

Ace All Your Classes

A Million Dollars

Wield All Magic

Win a Singing Competition

Ability to Freeze Time

True Love's Kiss

Impressive Kung Fu Skills

No Homework Ever Again

Everything You Touch Turns to Gold

To Become Royalty

Get Sold-Out Concert Tickets

Perfect Health

Trip to a Universal Studios Theme Park

Become a Stunt Double

World Peace

Go Viral on the Internet

To Live Forever

To Be a Famous Writer

A Dragon

All-Expenses Paid Trip to Japan

A Kitten

Unlimited Dumplings

Psychic Powers

Winner

Which DreamWorks character would you most like to challenge in your favorite video game?

Donkey

Hiccup

Megamind

Turbo

Yi

Skipper

Po

Puss In Boots

Tigress

Lord Farquaad

Poppy

Ruffnut

Jack Frost

Biggie

Tighten

Everest

Mr. Ping

Shrek

Kitty Softpaws

Captain Smek

Pinocchio

Wolf

Fishlegs

Rico

DJ Suki

Master Shifu

Goldilocks

Branch

RJ

Baby Bear

Stoick the Vast

Eep

Winner

In *Gift of the Night Fury*, Hiccup tries some Yaknog, but he's not the biggest fan. Which drink do you think Hiccup would like most?

Leche

Yak Milk

Eggnog

Fresh Water

Iced Tea

Hot Chocolate

Orange Juice

Beef Bone Broth

Fruit Punch

Sparkling Water

Apple Cider

Fish Stock

Green Juice

Protein Shake

Watermelon Juice

Raspberry Slushie

The Happily Ever After Potion

Hot Tea

Cherry Soda

Peach Juice

Oat Milk

Lemonade

Strawberry Milkshake

Coconut Water

Kombucha

Root Beer Float

Ginger Ale

Peanut Butter Smoothie

Vanilla Malt

Cookies and Cream Milkshake

Prune Juice

Chocolate Milk

Winner

Write in your own:

With the following prompt, fill in your own Bracketivity!

Which DreamWorks character would you
most want to be friends with?

Winner

Biggie is going to a costume party! What's the best costume?

Bee

Ogre

Mechanic

Mermaid

Kitty Softpaws

Ghost

Alien

Firefighter

Vampire

Sloth

Werewolf

Smoove Move

Dragon

Penguin

Princess Fiona

Megamind

Fairy

Alex the Lion

Zombie

Chef

Lord Farquaad

Street Fighter

Metro Man

Football Player

King Julien

Doctor

Punk Rocker

Panda

Ballerina

Witch

Butterfly

Cat

Winner

Now it's your turn!

Now that you're a pro at Bracketivities, you're all-knowing, just like the Magic Mirror. Turn the page and make your own Bracketivities. You can also use this page to jot down any notes you have.

_____   _____
_____   _____
_____   _____
_____   _____
_____   _____
_____   _____
_____   _____
_____   _____
_____   _____
_____   _____
_____   _____
_____   _____
_____   _____
_____   _____
_____   _____
_____   _____
_____   _____

Winner

Winner

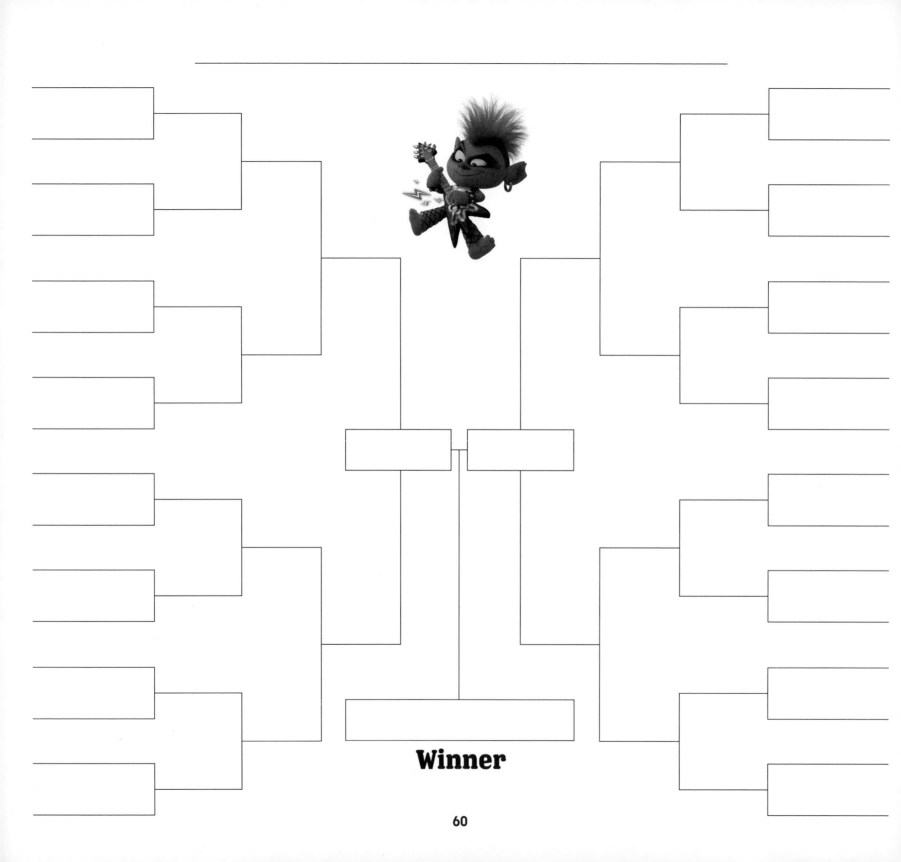

Winner

Winner

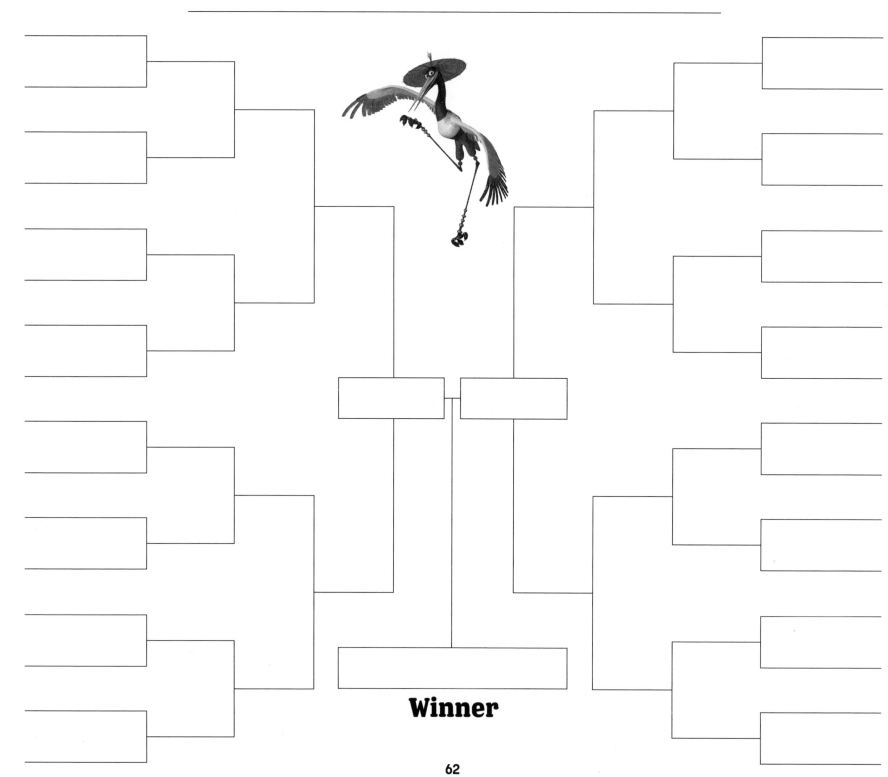

Winner

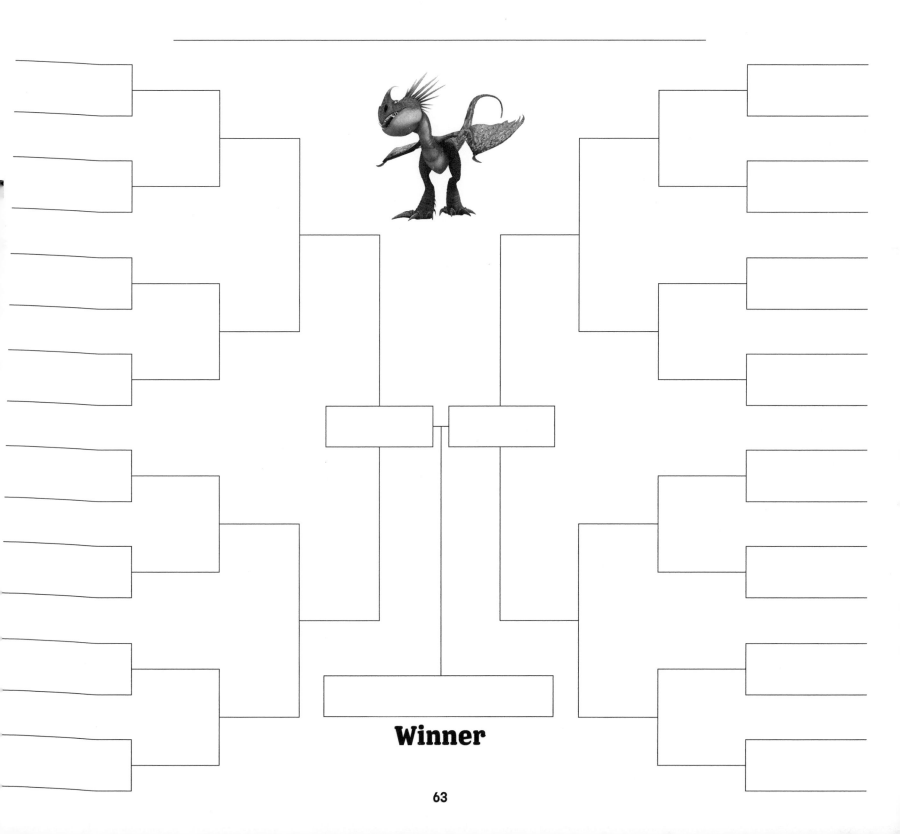

Winner

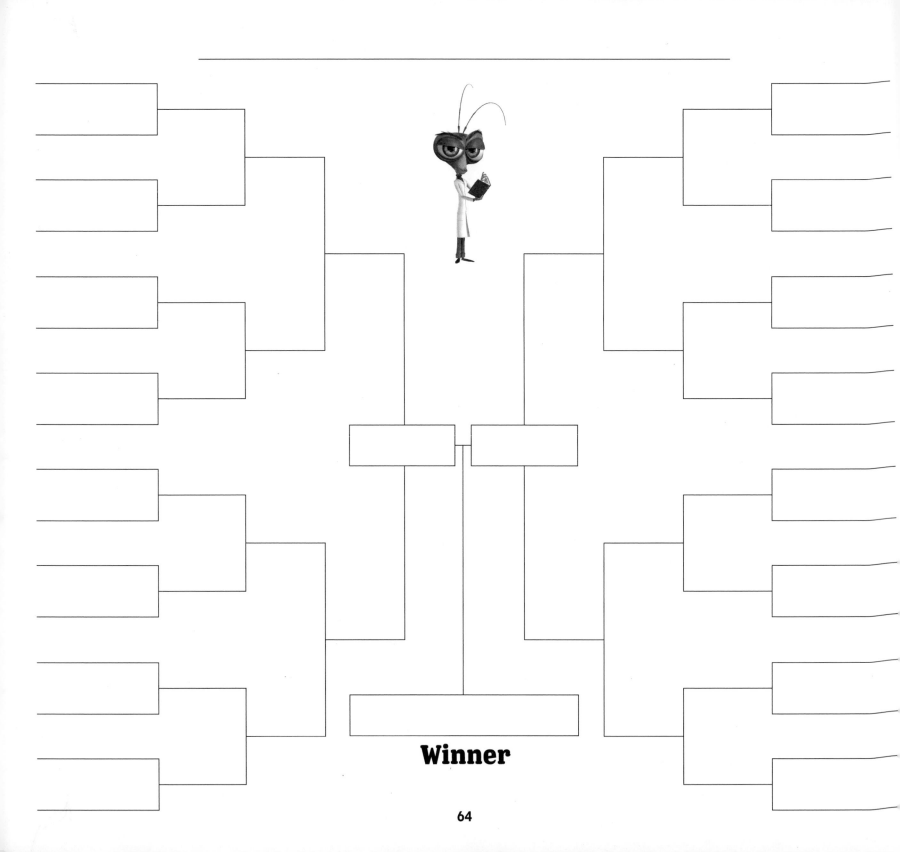

Winner